Fred
The Monarch

A Tale of
Transformation
& Hope

Delila Olsson

This book is dedicated to Earth
and her creatures, our very
best teachers.

Introduction

Do you remember when the pandemic began in 2020? Life changed a lot. Even though we still had birthdays and holidays, everything suddenly felt different. We wore masks, we rarely gathered, and only in small safe groups. We kept our distance to keep each other safe.

Like many people, I sometimes felt sad, missing my friends and, most of all, missing the children at the Montessori school where I work as an administrator.

Glimmers of hope can arrive at unexpected times, though. This is a story about one of those glimmers that grew into a whole story of hope, in the form of a tiny caterpillar who taught me that full-of-life things can, and do, burst forth even during life's most difficult times.

During the pandemic I kept a daily journal, and some of those entries became the story of Fred.

I hope you enjoy our story as much as I enjoyed writing it.

5 OCTOBER:

A Gift!

Yesterday was a very special day because my friend, Maryse, came to visit. To keep each other safe, we sat outside, far apart, with masks on. It wasn't the same as sitting side by side, but it was still great. We told stories about our lives, and we laughed a lot.

We also talked about how Earth and her creatures just keep going, even during a pandemic. And she reminded me how Monarch butterflies carry on.

Then she gave me the most wonderful gift: a milkweed plant from her garden in California, for me to plant in my garden in Oregon. Milkweed is the main diet of Monarchs, Maryse explained, and this plant would attract Monarch butterflies to my garden next spring.

As Maryse carefully handed me the potted plant, we noticed a tiny caterpillar munching away on a milkweed leaf. Aha! A Monarch caterpillar!

We both felt so excited to see the tiny caterpillar!

If the caterpillar survived, Maryse explained, it could grow to be the size of my little finger within about a month. Then it would form a chrysalis, and later emerge as a Monarch butterfly.

As soon as I said goodbye to Maryse, I started reading about the life cycle of Monarch butterflies.

6 OCTOBER:
Introducing Fred the Monarch

I placed the milkweed plant, with the tiny caterpillar, in the middle of my dining room table so I could easily observe its growth. And I decided to give the caterpillar a name: Fred.

Monarch is a word for a kind of butterfly, but it also means "King." Long ago, a man called Frederick the Great was the monarch of an area in what we now know as Europe.

I thought Frederick the Great would make a good name for a caterpillar, especially one that I hoped would survive to become a butterfly.

I am calling him "Fred" for short.

7 OCTOBER:

Preparing a Home

When I was a little girl, I often saw Monarch butterflies sailing gracefully through the air with their beautiful orange and black wings. I remember skipping through my garden, following the path of a Monarch. But nowadays, it is rare to see a Monarch where I live in Oregon.

I learned that Monarch butterflies don't fly when it's colder than 55 degrees. This caterpillar came from Santa Cruz, California, where temperatures are warmer in fall and winter than the ones we have here.

Which means it could be shocking or even fatal for Fred to spend the night outside here in Portland, in October.

Therefore, Fred will have to stay indoors.

Very Busy, Very Wise Caterpillar

Fred eats a lot. Every morning, I count the number of milkweed leaves remaining.

Maryse guessed that one milkweed plant would be enough to feed Fred for the duration of his caterpillar phase of life. Considering how quickly he is consuming the leaves, though, I am not so sure about that!

Watching Fred grow has become my favorite pastime.

14 OCTOBER:

Growing and Becoming

It has been 10 days since Fred the caterpillar became the centerpiece of my dining room table. He has already grown to 10 times his original size, and he spends all of his time either eating or resting. When he's awake, his tiny feet move in tandem, eating and growing and eating some more. He is rapidly chewing through the leaves of the milkweed plant where he has lived since birth.

There is no structure surrounding the plant, so Fred could wander away at any time. But he remains, moving from leaf to leaf, solely focused on growing and becoming.

I'm learning a lot by observing Fred. I am so glad he is here!

15 OCTOBER:
Possibilities

I am feeling very excited about the possibility of a butterfly being born right in the middle of my dining room table!

Because Fred is eating so many milkweed leaves so quickly—he is basically eating all day and all night—I am concerned that he might run out of leaves before he can form a chrysalis. I keep wondering why he has not made his way over to the larger stem, which contains many more leaves than the one he is on now.

Don't Mess with Mother Nature!

Fred probably does not need my help, but I kept thinking he could be feasting on the bigger milkweed stem, so I gently positioned an old wooden ruler next to his body. I hoped he would climb on board so I could transfer him to the larger milkweed stem.

Fred recoiled and remained frozen in that position for a long time, as if to say, "Don't mess with Mother Nature!" He now appears to be contentedly gnawing away at the stem.

Even though Fred is fully equipped for his task of becoming, sometimes I imagine that I know what is best for him.

Sometimes we all think we know what is best for others but, as Fred is teaching me, most of the time we are wrong about that.

17 OCTOBER:
Fred Eats. A lot.

I read that during the caterpillar stage, the creature increases 2000 times its original size. It is amazing to witness!

I placed the wooden ruler across the top of the milkweed pot to make a bridge, and since my last writing, Fred, the very hungry caterpillar, has made his way across it to reach the larger stalk of leaves. In the past two days, he has consumed almost all the leaves I expected to last for the rest of his caterpillar incarnation. And he has, again, almost doubled in size.

I am worried about Fred running out of food because now it's too late in the year to find milkweed plants in the wild. So I put a call out to some friends who have been following Fred's story.

Operation Milkweed

Just as things were looking rather hopeless for Fred, my friend Shirley came to the rescue! The milkweed plant in her garden had already lost most of its leaves after the first frost but, in a tricky and perfectly timed operation, Shirley was able to salvage a small bunch of leaves for Fred.

Shirley also helped me create an enclosed mesh butterfly home for Fred, who had thus far been grazing, unfettered, on the dining room table.

I did not like the idea of putting Fred in a cage, because I believe animals should be able to move freely, but he is growing so fast and, as he grows, he poops... a lot! When he was tiny, all those little green poop pellets fell into the pot or saucer holding the milkweed plant but, more recently, the pellets have begun to scatter all over my dining room table. Ew. Gross.

Also, as Fred prepares for his body to enter the chrysalis stage, he will need a safe place to attach, so we added a couple of small fir branches, collected from my front yard, to the enclosure.

According to my research, the Monarch caterpillar stage lasts between 7 and 17 days. Fred has been with me for 15 days, so he must be getting close to making his big transition.

19 OCTOBER:
Transformation Takes Time

Fred spent today devouring most of the remaining milkweed leaves in his enclosure. A little while ago I discovered he had left the plant, which means the search has begun for a place to attach, hang, and enter his next phase of life: the chrysalis stage.

The fir branches are easy to reach from the plant where Fred has lived for the past 16 days. But Fred had his own plan: he climbed up the netted side of the butterfly house and, for a long time, he lay still in the upside-down position, on the ceiling.

I've read it takes about 18 hours for the Monarch caterpillar to completely reform itself as a chrysalis, so it occurred to me that this might be the last time I get to observe Fred in caterpillar form; by morning this miraculous creature may have entered the next stage of life.

If everything happens on schedule, Fred the Monarch will emerge in his butterfly form in around 8 to 15 days.

Tonight, I am feeling grateful for the unexpected blessing of my caterpillar friend, and hoping that he will remind us all of the amazing energy of transformation. Things have been very difficult for so many of us since the pandemic began, and I think we could all use the reminder.

Caterpillar to Chrysalis

Fred stayed in the upside-down position on the ceiling of the net enclosure for about 36 hours. I noticed, late last night, he had dropped into a "J" formation, anchored to the netting by a little pad of self-spun silk at the back of his body.

He was completely still and remained so for most of the day. Every hour or so I checked on his progress, hoping to witness Fred's miraculous transformation from caterpillar to chrysalis. But sometimes nature's most magical moments happen in private, and in this case, I only got to observe the final quivering of Fred's transformation into a shimmering green chrysalis.

What's Going On In There?

Fred doesn't look anything like his caterpillar self! Now, Fred the chrysalis glistens like an iridescent jewel: he looks like a tiny, green time capsule! The color reminds me of the green glass cups from which I often sip my morning coffee.

The chrysalis stage is in an utterly magical process. Some of the inner changes will become visible closer to the time of Fred's emergence as a butterfly, but as I observe Fred's current state, I am eager to learn more about the process. What exactly is going on in there?

I learned that the chrysalis, while appearing to be at rest, is in fact hosting the most active, creative phase of the butterfly's becoming. The caterpillar's body begins to digest itself from the inside out, eventually turning almost entirely to liquid as it reforms itself as a butterfly. Inside the chrysalis, the old caterpillar body is broken down into imaginal cells, which are the ones that create the process of metamorphosis—a beautiful word for change—from caterpillar to butterfly. These cells form the wings, antennae, and other organs of the butterfly.

"*Imaginal*" seems to me the perfect name for cells that build butterflies! It reminds me that sometimes we have to imagine things before we can make them happen.

29 OCTOBER:
Like Magic!

Like an honored guest, Fred hangs from the butterfly enclosure on my dining room table. Even my cat, Staccato, is in awe.

Subtle changes are becoming visible from the outside as a butterfly is formed within. Even though this is the way all caterpillars become butterflies, to me it seems like magic!

30 OCTOBER:
The Family of Things

For such a small creature, Fred is teaching me so much.

I have been thinking about how all things follow a cycle of life and today, All Saint's Day, I have been thinking a lot about the ancestors in my Scandinavian family.

So, as I do every year, I carried my basket into the garden and gathered some greens and flowers and put them in a vase to honor my human family. I set the vase beside Fred's enclosure and said a prayer of gratitude for the mysterious way Fred fits into my family of things.

31 OCTOBER:

There is a lot going on...

Today is Halloween, which falls on a full moon. During a pandemic. Of course, being a butterfly, Fred doesn't know anything about Halloween or pandemics.

Fred does know about how big things—good things—like transforming to a whole new being, for instance, can happen when we are quiet, patient, and focused on our own growth.

That seems like a useful lesson for humans too.

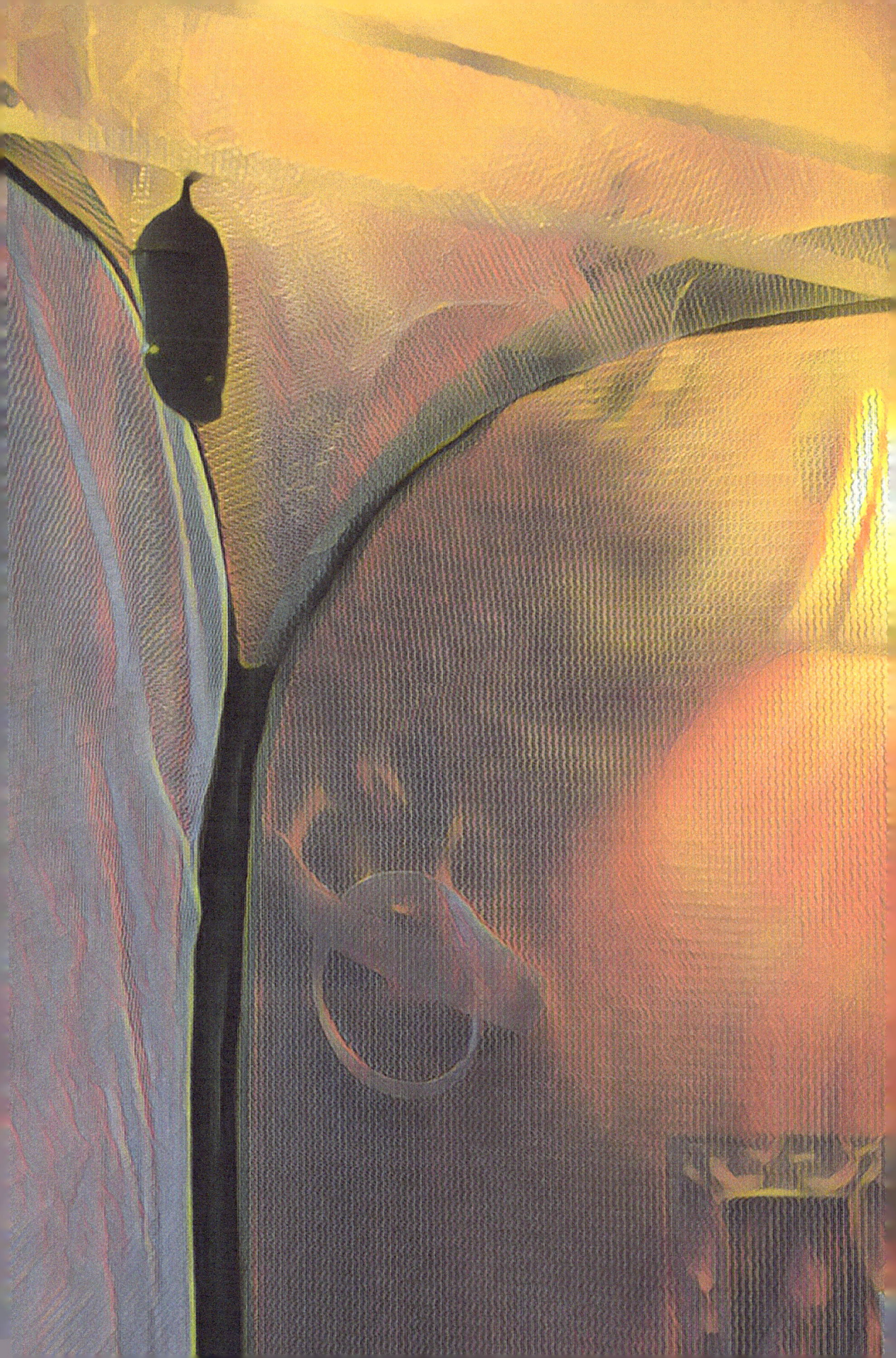

2 NOVEMBER:

Thinking about Transformation

While so many adults are concerned about the pandemic, I find Fred to be a calming, hopeful influence in my life. Perhaps because, according to one of my Native American teachers, butterflies represent transformation. In other words, they remind us that all things change.

Change doesn't only happen to butterflies; it happens to people too.

What changes would you like to see in yourself? In your life?

3 NOVEMBER:
Change is Becoming Visible!

Every day, I snap a couple of photos. From one day to the next, they reveal only slight changes in color and form. But today, Fred's wings are becoming faintly visible as his big transformation draws nearer.

His inner wings, while not yet outstretched and ready to fly, are preparing for the task.

Waiting is hard.

4 NOVEMBER:

Waiting...

This morning I expected to discover that Fred had become a butterfly. But Fred is still doing his invisible work, staying true to his own sense of timing, no matter what I think it should be.

Nature follows her own timetable.

The only thing to do is wait.

5 NOVEMBER:
Gathering Nature's Wisdom

Today it is still not clear when Fred the Monarch will emerge in his butterfly form. But I arrived home to find that Fred had changed profoundly since I left this morning. The orange and black wings of the butterfly are now clearly visible through the thinning chrysalis!

Perhaps Fred will fly soon.

6 NOVEMBER:
Today is The Day!

This morning, Fred was poised to take a new form. His wings were clearly visible, and almost ready to fly!

When I arrived home from school, I ran to the table to find Fred, newly emerged as a Monarch butterfly, holding fast to the empty chrysalis, his wings still damp. I felt a little sad at having missed the great transition, but it looks like Fred prefers to carry out his big transformative processes in private. I guess I can understand that.

I wonder how those big wings once fit into a chrysalis that was no bigger than the top segment of my pinky finger!

Fred has now left the chrysalis and moved onto the top of the netting, where he slowly opens and closes his newly formed wings. Wings that, in the next few days, will carry the butterfly to a new destination.

It is another miracle rippling out into a universe made of miracles.

7 NOVEMBER:
We Fly!

Fred is a California butterfly, and I can't release him into my yard, since Oregon is too cold and he wouldn't survive. As I make plans for the next leg of Fred's journey, I have put out a call for creative solutions and suggestions from my online community. I hope someone might have a nice warm greenhouse where a beautiful Monarch could winter over, or someone headed to California could take my butterfly on a road trip!

8 NOVEMBER:
A Lesson in Trust

Fred has a new home!

I wanted Fred to be able to fly free for as long as his wings would carry him but I knew that releasing him into nature here, in the autumn cold, would mean certain death.

Luckily, friends helped search for greenhouse possibilities, sought ride shares for Fred to points south, and contributed nectar sources for Fred's temporary tabletop home.

One dear friend introduced me to Virginia, a former zookeeper and animal enthusiast who graciously offered to host Fred in her indoor garden oasis. There, Fred will have sources of nectar, water, and plenty of space for flying!

It takes a village to raise a Monarch and I am so grateful for the helpful humans in my village.

Fred's journey, from Santa Cruz to Portland, from caterpillar to chrysalis to butterfly, shows us how to patiently trust nature's process. Fred is a real-life example of the transformative process that is always at work, even when we cannot see it.

Tonight, Fred the Monarch is feasting on pineapple sage and juicy orange slices. We can never know what will happen next, but we can know that we will get through it together because, like Fred, we are constantly changing and growing.

9 NOVEMBER:
Firsts and Lasts

This morning, I thought about how many people helped me take care of Fred, and how we are also taking care of each other.

Later, Staccato and I said our goodbyes to Fred, and I took him to his new home with Virginia. There won't be any other butterflies there, but there will be dogs and guinea pigs and hundreds of plants. And Fred will fly freely for as long as his wings will carry him.

I cried a lot today, feeling sad about saying goodbye to Fred.

He showed up in my life at the perfect time, to cheer me up and teach me how, like butterflies, we can choose to accept that change is a part of life, and that we all have the potential for metamorphosis. It can't be rushed—it takes the time it takes—but change can still happen.

13 NOVEMBER:
Transformation is Big Work

Today I got an update from Virginia, who reports that our butterfly friend is thriving in his new habitat, feasting on homemade nectar and flying around the indoor garden. She wrote, "He's definitely enjoying my mini jungle!"

If Fred's path had unfolded as nature intended, he would have been a chrysalis in California, and then he would have transformed there and joined the Monarch migration to Mexico. But sometimes things do not go as planned. Instead, he ended up living much of his life on my dining room table. Still, Fred's detour became my blessing and inspired me to write this book about change.

Transformation is big work. Thank goodness we do not have to do it alone.

Here's to the journey...and to all the ways we help each other through it.

AUTHOR
Delila Olsson

As a lifelong Montessori educator, Delila Olsson believes children need to connect deeply with nature and nature stories to understand their place in the family of things. She lives in a cottage in Lake Oswego, Oregon, with her cat, Staccato, and enjoys traipsing through the local rainforest or digging in her little garden. *Fred the Monarch: A Tale of Transformation & Hope* is her first book in a series of illuminating animal stories. Find her online at DelilaOlsson.com.

COVER ARTIST
Rosa Vela Sachs

Rosa and Delila recognized each other's spark and humor across the room at a small, Montessori school in Dallas, Texas. That was three decades ago, and they've been friends ever since. One of nine children, Rosa learned early that entertainment was possible anywhere there was a stick and a surface on which to draw. Her creativity knows no bounds.